WITHDRAWN

JILL BIDEN
Making a Difference as First Lady

By Katie Kawa

KidHaven
PUBLISHING

People Who Make a Difference

Published in 2023 by
KidHaven Publishing, an Imprint of Greenhaven Publishing, LLC
29 E. 21st Street
New York, NY 10010

Copyright © 2023 KidHaven Publishing, an Imprint of Greenhaven Publishing, LLC.

All rights reserved. No part of this book may be reproduced in any form without permission in writing from the publisher, except by a reviewer.

Designer: Deanna Paternostro
Editor: Katie Kawa

Photo credits: Cover, pp. 7, 11 mark reinstein/Shutterstock.com; p. 5 American Photo Archive/Alamy Stock Photo; p. 9 Sipa USA/Alamy Stock Photo; p. 13 Everett Collection/Shutterstock.com; p. 15 Crush Rush/Shutterstock.com; p. 17 photowalking/Shutterstock.com; p. 18 Spike Johnson/Shutterstock.com; p. 20 GM/Current Affairs/Alamy Stock Photo; p. 21 T.Sumaetho/Shutterstock.com.

Library of Congress Cataloging-in-Publication Data

Names: Kawa, Katie, author.
Title: Jill Biden : making a difference as First Lady / Katie Kawa.
Other titles: Making a difference as First Lady
Description: New York : KidHaven Publishing, [2023] | Series: People who make a difference | Includes bibliographical references and index.
Identifiers: LCCN 2021058564 | ISBN 9781534541757 (library binding) | ISBN 9781534541733 (paperback) | ISBN 9781534541740 (set) | ISBN 9781534541764 (ebook)
Subjects: LCSH: Biden, Jill–Juvenile literature. | Presidents' spouses–United States–Biography–Juvenile literature. | Educators–United States–Biography–Juvenile literature.
Classification: LCC E918.B53 K39 2023 | DDC 973.934092 [B]–dc23/eng/20220120
LC record available at https://lccn.loc.gov/2021058564

Printed in the United States of America

CPSIA compliance information: Batch #CSKH23: For further information contact Greenhaven Publishing LLC, New York, New York at 1-844-317-7404.

Please visit our website, www.greenhavenpublishing.com. For a free color catalog of all our high-quality books, call toll free 1-844-317-7404 or fax 1-844-317-7405.

Find us on

CONTENTS

Many Ways to Make a Difference	4
In the Classroom	6
Becoming a Biden	8
Dr. Biden	10
Life as the Second Lady	12
A New Role	14
Joining Forces	16
Other Causes	18
Kindness in Hard Times	20
Glossary	22
For More Information	23
Index	24

MANY WAYS TO MAKE A DIFFERENCE

Dr. Jill Biden is a busy woman! She's a mother and a grandmother. She's a teacher. She's also the wife of Joseph R. Biden Jr.—the 46th president of the United States. That makes her the First Lady of the United States.

Throughout U.S. history, the First Lady has often chosen different causes to support and initiatives, or plans to help people, to lead. Jill Biden is no different. As First Lady, she helps military families and calls attention to the importance of education. Through hard work and kindness, Jill makes a big difference in the lives of her family members, students, and fellow Americans.

In Her Words

"Remember to always, always, be yourself."

— Speech to **graduates** from May 2015

Even after Joe Biden became president, Jill kept working as a teacher at a community college. That made her the first First Lady to keep her paying job after her husband became president.

IN THE CLASSROOM

Jill was born on June 3, 1951, in Hammonton, New Jersey, but she grew up just outside of Philadelphia, Pennsylvania, in a town called Willow Grove. Her full name when she was born was Jill Tracy Jacobs, and she was the oldest of five sisters.

Jill finished high school in 1969. She later went to college to study English at the University of Delaware. In 1976, Jill started teaching English at St. Mark's High School in Wilmington, Delaware. Helping her students succeed became an important part of Jill's life, and it would stay that way even after she met Joe.

In Her Words

"Growing up, I knew early what I wanted in life: a marriage like my parents', maybe kids, definitely a career [job]. Although things didn't necessarily happen in that order, I did get all three. But it wasn't always easy."

— Speech to graduates from May 2014

Jill grew up near Philadelphia, and she returned there in 2016 to give a speech at the Democratic National Convention. This is a meeting of members of the **Democratic Party** in which they formally announce who's going to run for president and vice president.

BECOMING A BIDEN

In 1975, Jill went on a blind date. The man she was meeting was a U.S. Senator with two young sons. His name was Joe Biden.

A few years before meeting Jill, Joe's wife and daughter died in a car accident. He's said that Jill helped put his family back together. Jill fell in love not just with Joe, but also with his two sons—Beau and Hunter. She married Joe on June 17, 1977. Then, in 1981, she gave birth to their daughter, Ashley. No matter how busy Joe and Jill were, they made time for their family—and that's still true today.

In Her Words

"How do you make a broken family whole? The same way you make a nation whole: with love and understanding and with small acts of kindness … We show up for each other in big ways and small ones again and again."

— Speech at the 2020 Democratic National Convention

Joe and Jill support each other, and they've helped each other reach their goals.

DR. BIDEN

While Joe continued his work in the Senate, Jill went back to school. She earned two **master's degrees**—one in education and one in English. These degrees helped her as she continued teaching. Jill taught at a hospital that helped young people who were struggling with their **mental** health. She also worked in high schools.

In 1993, Jill began teaching at Delaware Technical Community College. She's taught at community colleges ever since then. Jill also continued her own education. In 2007, she earned her doctorate—the highest degree a person can earn—in education from the University of Delaware. This was when she became Dr. Jill Biden!

In Her Words

"For me, being a teacher isn't just what I do—it's who I am."

— Speech at the 2012 Democratic National Convention

Delaware was the state the Bidens called home for many years, and it was the state Joe served as a member of the U.S. Senate. Jill taught at schools in Delaware for much of her career.

LIFE AS THE SECOND LADY

In 2009, Jill's life changed in a big way when Joe became vice president of the United States. Joe worked closely with President Barack Obama, and Jill worked with First Lady Michelle Obama too. Over time, they became close friends.

Jill continued to teach even as she took on a new role, or job, as Second Lady—the title given to the wife of the vice president. She began working at Northern Virginia Community College after she and Joe moved to Washington, D.C. Jill also wrote a children's book. *Don't Forget, God Bless Our Troops* came out in 2012.

In Her Words

"When I became second lady—and there was so much I wanted to do—I always said, 'I will never waste this **platform**.'"

— Interview with *Vogue* magazine from June 2021

Shown here are Barack and Michelle Obama and Jill and Joe Biden on the night Barack won the U.S. presidential election in 2008. Barack won again in 2012, and Joe worked with him as vice president for four more years.

A NEW ROLE

Many people thought Joe would run for president in 2016. However, he and Jill had just lost their son Beau to **cancer** in 2015. Joe knew he needed time to heal, so he didn't run for president that year. Jill stayed busy teaching and writing a book about her life called *Where the Light Enters: Building a Family, Discovering Myself*. It came out in 2019.

By 2020, Joe was ready to run for president. He won the election, and Jill officially became First Lady in January 2021. Even with her new role, Jill kept teaching at Northern Virginia Community College. She likes making a difference in the lives of her students.

In Her Words

"Growing up takes some stepping up."

— Speech to graduates from May 2014

Jill supported her husband before the 2020 presidential election by giving speeches about all the good things he would do for Americans.

15

JOINING FORCES

Jill supports many different causes as First Lady, but one of the initiatives that's closest to her heart is called Joining Forces. Jill started Joining Forces with Michelle Obama during her time as Second Lady, and she brought it back when she became First Lady.

Joining Forces helps military families with education, jobs, and care for both their **physical** and mental health. Jill knows what it's like to have a loved one in the military. Her father had served in the U.S. Navy. In addition, Beau Biden served his country in Iraq as part of the Delaware Army National Guard.

In Her Words

"As a proud military mom myself, I know that when you have a family member who is in the military, the whole family serves too."

— Comments at the start of Military Family Month in October 2014

Taking care of the people who serve in the U.S. military and their families is very important to Jill. She's shown here visiting soldiers in the hospital.

17

OTHER CAUSES

Jill makes a difference in the lives of military families through Joining Forces, but that's not the only way she's helping people as First Lady. She's a strong supporter of community colleges and has helped make sure teachers have a voice in the White House. She also works to raise awareness about the importance of education for all people—and especially for women and girls.

In addition, both Joe and Jill are active in the fight against cancer. Jill started an initiative to teach girls in high school about the importance of finding certain kinds of cancer early enough to treat.

In Her Words

"I feel every day, like … What could I give up? That I would want to give up? Nothing. If anything, I feel like adding more things, but I know it's not possible, because you want to stay centered, because you want to do things well. And there's so much to do."

— Interview with *Vogue* magazine from June 2021

The Life of Jill Biden

1951
Jill Tracy Jacobs is born in New Jersey on June 3.

1969
Jill finishes high school.

1975
Jill meets Joe Biden.

1976
Jill starts teaching at St. Mark's High School in Wilmington, Delaware.

1977
Joe and Jill get married.

1993
Jill starts teaching at a community college in Delaware.

2007
Jill earns her doctorate from the University of Delaware and becomes Dr. Jill Biden.

2009
Jill becomes Second Lady when Joe becomes vice president.

2012
Jill's children's book, *Don't Forget, God Bless Our Troops*, comes out, and Joe is elected to another term as vice president.

2015
Jill and Joe's son Beau dies of cancer.

2019
Jill's book *Where the Light Enters: Building a Family, Discovering Myself* comes out.

2021
Jill becomes First Lady when Joe becomes president.

Jill Biden has worked hard her whole life to make a difference in the world around her.

KINDNESS IN HARD TIMES

Jill Biden became First Lady during a scary time for Americans. The **COVID-19 pandemic** had made life hard for many people, especially teachers and students. Jill showed her support for them, and she worked to make sure schools were as safe as possible during this time.

Dr. Jill Biden is able to help millions of people through her role as First Lady. However, she was also making a difference long before she moved to the White House. She believes that simple acts of kindness can make the world a better place, and that's something anyone can do!

In Her Words

"Show kindness to others with your time, but most of all with your heart."

— Speech to graduates from May 2015

Be Like Jill Biden!

If you like helping other people learn, **volunteer** as a **tutor** at your school.

Raise money for groups that fight cancer.

Learn as much as you can about subjects and causes that matter to you.

Work hard in school, and show your friends that it's important to care about your education.

If there are kids from military families at your school, reach out to them, and make them feel included in your school community.

Raise money to help military families and people who've served in the military.

Support your family members and friends when they're working toward an important goal. Speak up about the goals you have and the things you want to do too.

Jill Biden makes a difference in many ways, and these are just some examples of how you can be more like her.

GLOSSARY

cancer: A sometimes deadly sickness in which cells grow in a way they should not, often forming tumors, or growths, that harm the body.

COVID-19 pandemic: An event that began in China in 2019 in which a disease that causes breathing problems, a fever, and other health issues spread rapidly around the world and made millions of people sick in a short period of time.

Democratic Party: One of the two main political parties—groups with different ideas about how the government should work—in the United States.

graduate: A person who has finished the required course of study in a school.

master's degree: A title given to students following additional years of study at a college or university after receiving their bachelor's degree, which is generally given after four years of study.

mental: Relating to the mind.

physical: Relating to the body.

platform: An opportunity to talk publicly.

tutor: A private teacher or someone who helps another person with schoolwork.

volunteer: To do something to help because you want to do it.

FOR MORE INFORMATION

WEBSITES

Dr. Jill Biden

www.whitehouse.gov/administration/dr-jill-biden/

The official White House website has facts about Jill Biden's life and the work she's doing as First Lady.

NBC News: "Watch Jill Biden's Full Speech At The 2020 DNC"

www.youtube.com/watch?v=_sT9lolkVaU

Visit YouTube to watch Jill Biden's speech at the 2020 Democratic National Convention, which was about her life and her husband.

BOOKS

Andrews, Elizabeth. *Jill Biden: Educator & First Lady of the United States*. North Mankato, MN: Abdo Kids, 2022.

Biden, Jill. *Don't Forget, God Bless Our Troops*. New York, NY: Simon & Schuster Books for Young Readers, 2012.

Neuenfeldt, Elizabeth. *Jill Biden: Educator*. Minnetonka, MN: Bellwether Media, 2022.

Publisher's note to educators and parents: Our editors have carefully reviewed these websites to ensure that they are suitable for students. Many websites change frequently, however, and we cannot guarantee that a site's future contents will continue to meet our high standards of quality and educational value. Be advised that students should be closely supervised whenever they access the Internet.

INDEX

B

Biden, Ashley, 8
Biden, Beau, 8, 14, 16, 19
Biden, Hunter, 8
Biden, Joe, 4, 5, 6, 8, 9, 10, 11, 12, 13, 14, 18, 19

C

cancer, 14, 18, 19, 21
community colleges, 5, 10, 12, 14, 18, 19

D

doctorate, 10, 19
Don't Forget, God Bless Our Troops, 12, 19

F

First Lady, 4, 5, 14, 16, 18, 19, 20

H

high schools, 6, 10, 18, 19

J

Joining Forces, 16, 18

O

Obama, Barack, 12, 13
Obama, Michelle, 12, 13, 16

S

Second Lady, 12, 16, 19

T

teaching, 4, 5, 6, 10, 12, 14, 19

U

University of Delaware, 6, 10, 19
U.S. Senate, 8, 10, 11

W

Where the Light Enters: Building a Family, Discovering Myself, 14, 19